From the stars in the sky . . .

to the fish in the sea.

Because of you the sun glows . . .

you brighten up the shadows.

Because of you I enjoy each minute . . .

of life's adventures, the sky's the limit.

Because of you I've learnt how to care . . .

about our world and the people there.

Because of you I can have fun . . .

enjoying life out in the sun.

Because of you I fight the bugs . . .

you also give the greatest hugs.

Because of you the swallows sing . . .

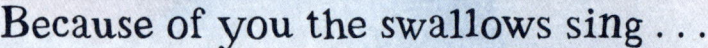

you are the kite that lifts my string.

Because of you there is no rain . . .

you're always there to ease the pain.

who'll be there to help me grow.

Because of you I'll take a chance . . .

you're always there to laugh and dance.

Because of you I don't feel cold . . .

you give me strength and make me bold.

Because of you I've learnt to see . . .

all the reasons I can be me.

You always make my world seem new.

Everything is better because of you.

First published by **FROM YOU TO ME LTD**, in February 2023.

For a full range of all our titles where gifts can also be personalised, please visit

WWW.FROMYOUTOME.COM

FROM YOU TO ME are committed to a sustainable future for our business, our customers and our planet. This book is printed and bound in China on FSC®certified paper.

Text & Illustrations Copyright © 2023 Robert McPhillips

All rights reserved. No part of this publication may be reproduced, stored in a retrieval system, or transmitted in any form or by any means electronic, mechanical, photocopying, recording, or otherwise, without the prior written permission of the copyright owner who can be contacted via the publisher at the above website address.

3 5 7 9 11 13 15 14 12 10 8 6 4 2

Copyright © 2023 **FROM YOU TO ME LTD**

ISBN 978-1-907860-89-8

FROM YOU TO ME LTD, STUDIO 100, THE OLD LEATHER FACTORY
GLOVE FACTORY STUDIOS, HOLT, WILTSHIRE, BA14 6RJ, UK